Little Bunny's
Book of Friends

Little Bunny's Book of Friends

Steve Smallman

This book belongs to:

_____

_____

_____

GRAFFEG

When it feels like your ears
are beginning to flop

and all of the bounce has gone
out of your hop,

When everything's driving you
right round the bend,

You know what you need?
What you need is...

...a friend.

Friends can be big,
Friends can be small.
The size or the shape
doesn't matter at all.

Friends are the ones
you can always rely on
when you need a hug or
a shoulder to cry on.

They make you feel safe
when you're lost or alone,

And listen and nod while you have
a good moan.

And when things
are going surprisingly well,
Your friends are the ones
that you can't wait to tell!

It's nice to have friends you can
share all your dreams with,

Or meet up and eat up enormous ice creams with!

Friends tell the truth when
it needs to be heard,

And know when it's best
if they don't say a word.

Friends never judge you or
want you to change,
They don't mind if you're just
a little bit strange.

You can just be yourself,
you don't need to pretend.
You'll be the best 'you'
you can be with a friend.

And the way to keep friends
who do all this for you,

Is to make sure that you're
a good friend to them too!

I may not be big and
I may not be clever,
but I know we'll be good friends...

... for ever and ever!

Steve Smallman

Steve Smallman has been writing and illustrating children's books for over 40 years. The author of *Smelly Peter the Great Pea Eater* (winner of the Sheffield Children's Book Award 2009) and *The Lamb Who Came for Dinner* (shortlisted for the Red House Children's Book Award and read by Meatloaf on CITV's *Bookaboo*), he received the Sheffield Children's Book Award again in 2019 for *Cock-a-Doodle Poo!*. Steve started working as an illustrator while he was still at art college, then, after about 20 years, decided to have a go at writing stories of his own. He has so far written over 100 books, with more on the way.

'*Little Bunny's Book of Thoughts* started with a doodle in my sketchbook. I was trying out a different technique using a soft pencil on a grainy textured paper. Without much conscious thought on my part, a worried little bunny appeared in a makeshift boat. I posted the drawing on social media and it seemed to strike a chord with so many people! So I drew more bunny pictures using different facial expressions and scenarios and soon had quite a collection. Put together they seemed to show an emotional journey for the little bunny that people could relate to. I added a minimal text to help bunny on his way and with the help of Graffeg, this book was born!'

The Little Bunny's Book of Thoughts

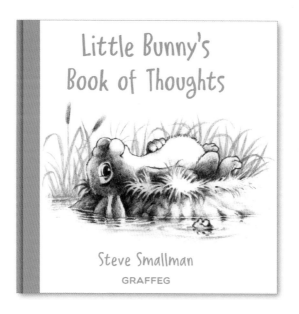

When everything feels like a challenge, take time to stop and breathe with Little Bunny's book of calm, quiet mindfulness.

Author Steve Smallman, Publication November 2020
HB, 48pp, 150 x 150mm, £6.99, ISBN 9781913134259
Published by Graffeg

Little Bunny's Book of Friends
Published in Great Britain in 2021 by Graffeg
Limited.

Written and illustrated by Steve Smallman
copyright © 2021. Designed and produced by
Graffeg Limited copyright © 2021.

Graffeg Limited, 24 Stradey Park Business
Centre, Mwrwg Road, Llangennech, Llanelli,
Carmarthenshire, SA14 8YP, Wales, UK.
Tel: 01554 824000. www.graffeg.com.

Steve Smallman is hereby identified as the author
of this work in accordance with section 77 of the
Copyrights, Designs and Patents Act 1988.

A CIP Catalogue record for this book is
available from the British Library.

ISBN 9781802580501

1 2 3 4 5 6 7 8 9

MIX
Paper from
responsible sources
FSC® C014138